This book
belongs to

Hazel and Juni
Love, Grandpa +
Grandma

A THANKFUL HEART IS A HAPPY HEART

52
Gratitude-
filled
Devotions
for Kids

BroadStreet
KIDS

BroadStreet Kids
Savage, Minnesota, USA

BroadStreet Kids is an imprint of BroadStreet Publishing Group, LLC.
Broadstreetpublishing.com

A THANKFUL HEART IS A HAPPY HEART DEVOTIONAL

© 2018 by BroadStreet Publishing®

ISBN 978-1-4245-5740-0 (hard cover)

ISBN 978-1-4245-5741-7 (e-book)

Devotional entries composed by Michelle Winger and Jeanna Harder.

Design by Chris Garborg | garborgdesign.com

Edited and compiled by Michelle Winger | literallyprecise.com

Printed in China.

18 19 20 21 22 23 24   7 6 5 4 3 2 1

INTRODUCTION

LORD, I will give thanks to you with all my heart.

I will tell about all the wonderful things you have done.

I will be glad and full of joy because of you.

Most High God, I will sing the praises of your name.

PSALM 9:1-2 NIRV

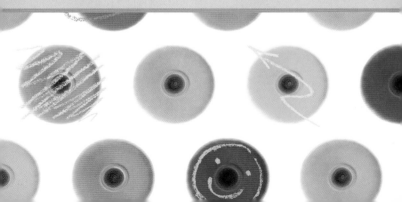

SMALL THINGS

I know how to live when I am poor, and I know how to live when I have plenty. I have learned the secret of being happy at any time in everything that happens, when I have enough to eat and when I go hungry, when I have more than I need and when I do not have enough. I can do all things through Christ, because he gives me strength.

PHILIPPIANS 4:12-13 NCV

We have favorite dinners, and meals that we don't like very much. Can you think of a favorite dinner of yours? Now think of someone who doesn't get dinners at all. That's pretty sad, right? It's good to be thankful for every meal that you get, even if you don't like it very much.

Paul, from the Bible, said that he was okay even when he was put in prison and didn't have very much of anything. That's because he was thankful for every little thing Jesus had given him. We can learn to be thankful no matter how much or how little we have.

Jesus, help me to be happy with whatever I have, even if it is only a little. I know I am very blessed to have food to eat when so many people around the world go without. Thank you for the food you have provided for me and my family.

DID YOU KNOW...

Some food looks like the part of the body they are good for!

- If you slice a carrot, it looks like an eye. Carrots help support blood flow to your eyes.

- A tomato has four chambers, just like the human heart. Tomatoes are full of lycopene which is great for your heart and your blood.

- Walnuts look like a brain! They develop neurotransmitters that help your brain work properly.

- Beans are shaped like kidneys. They help heal and strengthen your kidneys.

Act of Gratitude

I am thankful for the gift of food today.

Here's what I am going to do this week
to show how grateful I am.

I will thank everyone
for my meal, snack, or
desert. I will share
my food too.

WARMLY ACCEPTED

"The Father gives me the people who are mine.
Every one of them will come to me,
and I will always accept them."

JOHN 6:37 ICB

God's arms are always open to us, but sometimes we are afraid to go to him. We maybe don't feel like we deserve to have his love, or we are embarrassed by our sins. We think maybe God will turn away from us.

God says we are always welcome. There is nothing we could do that would cause him to reject us. Nothing can keep us from his love. He is waiting for us to run into his arms and feel his unconditional acceptance.

Thank you, God, for always loving me and drawing me closer to you. I am thankful that you accept me just the way that I am. Thank you for your love that encourages me to give up my bad habits and start making good decisions.

DID YOU KNOW...

Hugging is good for your health!

Hugging helps your nervous system and fights feeling of loneliness and fear. It makes you feel better about yourself, gets rid of unnecessary stress, and can cause you to feel appreciated. How? The simple act of hugging releases hormones in your body that make you feel better, lower your blood pressure, boost your immune system, reduce pain, and help you feel connected to others. Make sure you give someone a hug today!

Act of Gratitude

I am thankful for the gift of acceptance today.

Here's what I am going to do this week
to show how grateful I am.

I will give hugs and
make others feel loved
and feel like they belong.

THINKING LOVELY THINGS

Continue to think about the things that are good and worthy of praise. Think about the things that are true and honorable and right and pure and beautiful and respected.

PHILIPPIANS 4:8 ICB

Have you ever woken up from a bad dream? Sometimes yucky thoughts can get into our heads and it can be a little scary. Well, the words of the Bible tell us that there is something that we can do about bad thoughts. We can practice thinking about good things.

Try it now. Think of something that makes you laugh, or something that makes you feel happy. Think of something that makes you proud, or something that you are good at. Think of the things that you are thankful for in your life. See? You can think good thoughts!

God, when bad thoughts or pictures come into my mind, please remind me of all the lovely and right things that I can think about instead. Thank you that you can help me to turn my bad thoughts into good thoughts.

CHANGE ONE LETTER TO CREATE NEW WORDS AND TURN A POOR THOUGHT INTO A GOOD ONE.

POOR

POUR TRANSFER LIQUID INTO A CUP

POUT SULK

PORT PLACE FOR SHIPS TO DOCK

FORT A HIDING PLACE BUILT WITH BLANKETS

FOOT 12 INCHES

FOOD SOMETHING TO EAT

GOOD

Act of Gratitude

I am thankful for the ability to change my thoughts.

Here's what I am going to do this week
to show how grateful I am.

_____

_____

_____

_____

_____

_____

_____

_____

_____

MY ROCK

There isn't anyone holy like the LORD.
There isn't anyone except him.
There isn't any Rock like our God.
1 SAMUEL 2:2 NIRV

What is the biggest rock that you have seen? Did you try to pick it up? How heavy do you think it was? Rocks are strong and secure and the biggest ones are almost impossible to move.

When we start to worry, or become afraid, we can think about God like a rock. No matter what it is we are going through, he won't move. He will stay strong and steady right beside us. He is bigger than any of our troubles or fears. We can always trust him!

God, I am so thankful that you are my rock and my protection. You never leave me alone. You stay right next to me, strong and secure. Help me to remember to turn to you first in everything I do.

DID YOU KNOW...

The world's biggest rock is called Mount Augustus. It is in Australia. It is about 3,000 feet high and covers an area of about 18 square miles. That is one very big rock! It can take up to five hours to climb to the top of the rock and back down. As big as this rock is, it still doesn't even compare to how big God is!

Act of Gratitude

I am thankful that God is my rock! He is always with me.

Here's what I am going to do this week
to show how grateful I am.

_____

_____

_____

_____

_____

_____

_____

_____

_____

YOU CAN ALWAYS PRAY

First, I tell you to pray for all people.
Ask God for the things people need,
and be thankful to him. You should pray for kings
and for all who have authority. Pray for the leaders
so that we can have quiet and peaceful lives—
lives full of worship and respect for God.

1 Timothy 2:1-2 NLT

Do you ever wonder what to pray about? It can be hard to think of things. The Bible says that you can start by praying for people. You could ask God to bring happiness to children in other countries, or to help kids at school to be brave. You can pray for everyone you know, like your teachers, people at church, and your own family. We should even pray for our country's leaders so they can lead us better.

If you think of people, you will have a lot to pray for. God loves it when you spend time with him praying for others and sharing what is on your heart. He is always ready to listen to what you have to say.

God, thank you for giving me a way to communicate with you. Thank you for listening to me when I pray. Remind me to spend time praying to you each day. Help me to think of people that need prayer. I want to be a blessing to others and show them how much you care.

DID YOU KNOW?

We pray because we have a God who listens and wants to be a part of our lives. Prayer is also good for our health! Multiple scientific studies have shown that people who pray regularly are healthier and live longer lives. Perhaps its greatest medicinal benefit is that prayer reduces stress, and too much stress can make us sick. No wonder God wants us to pray. When we do, we strengthen both our spirit and our body.

Act of Gratitude

I am thankful that God listens to me when I pray!

Here's what I am going to do this week
to show how grateful I am.

_____

_____

_____

_____

_____

_____

_____

_____

_____

A BIG LIST OF THANKS

Let all that I am praise the LORD;
with my whole heart, I will praise his holy name.
Let all that I am praise the LORD;
may I never forget the good things he does for me.
He forgives all my sins
and heals all my diseases.
He redeems me from death
and crowns me with love and tender mercies.
He fills my life with good things.
My youth is renewed like the eagle's!

PSALM 103:1-5 NLT

If you tried to make a list of all the good things in your life, it would be pretty long. A warm bed, books to read, food to eat, toys to play with, friends at school, your pets at home. You could add so much more to that list!

The person who wrote this Bible verse was thankful for everything that God had given him. He was thankful for little things and big things. Remember to praise God for all the wonderful things in your life today.

God, I thank you for all the good things you have given me. Everything that I have that is good has come from you. Help me to remember just how blessed I am each day.

SEE IF YOU CAN THINK OF SOMETHING YOU ARE THANKFUL FOR STARTING WITH EACH LETTER OF THE ALPHABET.

A _____
B _____
C _____
D _____
E _____
F _____
G _____
H _____
I _____
J _____
K _____
L _____
M _____

N _____
O _____
P _____
Q _____
R _____
S _____
T _____
U _____
V _____
W _____
X _____
Y _____
Z _____

Act of Gratitude

I am thankful for every good thing in my life—
big things and small things!

Here's what I am going to do this week
to show how grateful I am.

_____

_____

_____

_____

_____

_____

_____

_____

_____

CHOOSING JOY

This is the day the L<small>ORD</small> has made.
We will rejoice and be glad in it.
P<small>SALM</small> 118:24 NLT

Some days are harder than others. The sun doesn't shine or the day just feels impossible. Thankfully, God has given us joy that doesn't depend on what's going on around us.

God's joy brings us out of hiding, and shows us the beautiful things around us in the middle of a sometimes dark and stormy world. God has given us his joy as a gift. We can choose to be joyful each day. Will you choose joy this week?

God, thank you that every day from you is a precious gift. Thank you that you are so full of joy and you offer me the same joy every morning I wake up. Help me to see your joy in everything I do and to choose joy when it's not so easy to see.

DID YOU KNOW...

Even if you don't feel like smiling, if you choose to put a smile on your face it can actually make you feel happier. Smiling on purpose changes the chemistry in your brain. When that happens, your behavior changes. Smiling can change your bad mood into a good one. It's really true—you can choose to be happy! Ask God for a lasting smile this week.

Act of Gratitude

I am thankful for the joy that God gives me!

Here's what I am going to do this week
to show how grateful I am.

_____

_____

_____

_____

_____

_____

_____

_____

_____

A BEAUTIFUL DAY

I will tell about the Lord's kindness.
And I will praise him for what he has done.
He has given many good things to us.
He has been very good to the people of Israel.
The Lord has shown mercy to us.
And he has been kind to us.

ISAIAH 63:7 NCV

God's goodness is great every day; his love is steady and it always fights for us. We can show God how thankful we are by remembering how good he is and telling others about what he has done for us.

Even when life isn't easy, the list of blessings God has given you is very long. This day is beautiful because God loves you and he is so good to you. Tell others about his kindness and mercy this week.

God, you are so good! Thank you for your kindness to me. Help me to share your love with others. I want them to see how wonderful you are. You have given me so much to be thankful for. Each day I want to remember your kindness and share it with others.

DID YOU KNOW...

A random act of kindness is something you do that cheers up the people around you. It's not something you do for yourself, but you can bet you will feel great once you've completed it! Here are some things you could do to show kindness.

Smile at someone you don't know

Hold a door open for someone behind you

Donate your gently used toys

Say thank you with a smile

Wash the dishes without being asked

Bring cookies to a neighbor

Act of Gratitude

I am thankful that God is so incredibly kind to me!

Here's what I am going to do this week
to show how grateful I am.

_____

_____

_____

_____

_____

_____

_____

_____

_____

STOP FOR THANKS

Enter his gates with thanksgiving
and his courts with praise;
give thanks to him and praise his name.
PSALM 100:4 NIV

Sometimes as soon as you wake up in the morning you feel busy: get dressed, get ready for school, eat breakfast, and get to the bus stop on time. It's important to do all of these things, but could you be forgetting something?

God wants us to remember him and thank him. It helps to be thankful toward God at the beginning of the day. Stopping to thank him in the morning gives you peace and joy that can last the whole day.

Loving Father, thank you for giving me another day on earth. Help me be thankful the moment I wake up. Teach me to start thanking you as soon as I start my day and to not stop thanking you until I go to bed at night. You have done so much for me; you deserve to be thanked continuously.

Make your way through this maze, stopping to give thanks when you find yourself in the middle.

Start here

Act of Gratitude

I am thankful to God every moment of every day!

Here's what I am going to do this week
to show how grateful I am.

_____

_____

_____

_____

_____

_____

_____

_____

_____

CREATIVITY

God created human beings in his image.
In the image of God he created them.
He created them male and female.
GENESIS 1:27 ICB

Sometimes we get jealous of the movie stars and rock stars on the covers of magazines. There are days when we want to be as good looking or popular as they are.

God did not create you to be just like everyone else. He created you to be special. What you are good at, someone else is not. Don't look at what other people are good at and feel bad about yourself. Instead, celebrate how wonderfully different God made you!

God, thank you for reminding me of how special you created me to be. You are the amazing Creator who has given me something special that no one else has. Help me to use what you have given me to bless others, and remind me to be thankful for who you made me to be.

Use the doodle on this page to create your own picture.

Act of Gratitude

I am thankful to God for making me wonderfully different!

Here's what I am going to do this week
to show how grateful I am.

_____

_____

_____

_____

_____

_____

_____

_____

_____

_____

WEATHER CONTROL

He covers the heavens with clouds,
prepares rain for the earth,
makes grass grow on the hills.
The LORD takes pleasure in those who fear him,
in those who hope in his steadfast love.

PSALM 147:8, 11 NRSV

How is the weather where you are? Has it been raining? Have you had a lot of sun? Is it too hot, or too cold, or is it just right? Do you find yourself complaining when the weather isn't exactly how you want it?

You can't control the weather, and you can't always control things happening to you. But you can control what to do when the weather is bad or when life is hard. Ask God to give you hope and peace, and be thankful that he knows exactly what kind of weather is right for today.

God, thank you that you are in control of the weather and of what happens in my life. Help me to be thankful that you care enough to help me grow in all situations. I want to be grateful when the sun is shining and when the skies are gray. You always know what is best.

DID YOU KNOW?

The coldest temperature ever recorded was a chilly -128.56°F.

There are about 2,000 thunderstorms around the world every minute.

The highest snowfall in one year was 1,224 inches in Mount Rainier, Washington in 1972.

The hottest temperature was recorded in Libya in 1922 when it reached 136.4°F.

Yuma, Arizona has over 4,000 hours of sunshine every year, which makes it the sunniest place on the planet!

The strongest wind ever recorded was 231 mph in New Hampshire.

The largest snowflake was measured at 15 inches wide and 7 inches thick. It fell in Montana on January 28, 1887.

Act of Gratitude

I am thankful to God for his ability to control the weather!

Here's what I am going to do this week
to show how grateful I am.

_____

_____

_____

_____

_____

_____

_____

_____

_____

_____

WORK HARD

People who refuse to work want things
and get nothing.
But the desires of people who work hard
are completely satisfied.

PROVERBS 13:4 NIRV

Working hard can actually make you feel really good. When you get a job done, you feel like you have done something helpful.

Sometimes when you are asked to do a job around the house, do you complain? You might take a long time to do the job. You might wish you were doing something else. The Bible says that you will be rewarded if you have a good attitude about doing work. Can you change your heart about doing jobs others have asked you to do? If you choose to be thankful, you might find that you begin enjoying the job!

God, help me to do the jobs that I am asked to do with joy and thankfulness. I know that you want me to have a good attitude toward helping others, and I know that you will reward me for working hard.

Unscramble the words below to figure out what kind of work you could do around the house to help out.

SWHA ISDEHS   _ _ _ _   _ _ _ _ _ _

PMEYT HRTSA   _ _ _ _ _   _ _ _ _ _

KEMA DBE   _ _ _ _   _ _ _

UMVUCA   _ _ _ _ _ _

OMW NLWA   _ _ _   _ _ _ _

AEKM NRDNEI   _ _ _ _   _ _ _ _ _ _

ELANC PU SYTO   _ _ _ _ _   _ _   _ _ _ _

REWTA LNATPS   _ _ _ _ _   _ _ _ _ _ _

Act of Gratitude

I am thankful to God for the ability to work hard.

Here's what I am going to do this week
to show how grateful I am.

_____

_____

_____

_____

_____

_____

_____

_____

_____

_____

CHEERLEADERS

Let us not give up meeting together. Some are in the habit of doing this. Instead, let us encourage one another with words of hope. Let us do this even more as you see Christ's return approaching.

HEBREWS 10:25 NIRV

What does the team mascot look like at your school? Do you have one, or know what it is? A mascot is someone dressed up like a character, and they are there to cheer on the sports team to help them win!

Good friends take the time to cheer each other on. They show up when their friends need them, and they say kind, thoughtful things. Be thankful for those friends in your life, and make sure you are a good friend too!

God, thank you for the people in my life who act like my cheerleaders. Thank you that they encourage me to make good decisions. Please help me to be positive and cheerful toward my friends and family so they will feel like I am cheering them on too.

Draw a line from beginning to end that passes through every box with a cheerleader in it once. The line can go up, down, left, or right, but not diagonally.

Act of Gratitude

I am thankful to God for the cheerleaders in my life.

Here's what I am going to do this week
to show how grateful I am.

_____

_____

_____

_____

_____

_____

_____

_____

FULL OF PEACE

"Peace I leave with you; my peace I give you. I do not give to you as the world gives. Do not let your hearts be troubled and do not be afraid."

JOHN 14:27 NIV

Have you ever seen a baby sleeping? Have you been outside and realized that everything was quiet? What about a time when you were quietly drawing and nobody was around to mess things up? These are moments of peace.

God loves peace! He loves it so much that he gives you peace. Sometimes life is too busy or too noisy or too scary. In those times, ask God for his peace in your heart and thank him for being the only source of true peace.

Thank you, God, for your gift of peace, I am so thankful that you settle and calm my heart in moments that feel busy, noisy, and scary. You are the only one who offers true peace and I gladly accept it.

DID YOU KNOW...

We spend very little of our awake time in silence. Too much noise is not good for our stress levels. Spending two minutes in silence is actually better for us than spending that same amount of time listening to "relaxing music." Sitting quietly helps lower our blood pressure and actually gives our brains a chance to restore themselves. So, take a break and sit in silence with God today. Your brain will thank you!

Act of Gratitude

I am thankful to God for his peace.

Here's what I am going to do this week
to show how grateful I am.

_____

_____

_____

_____

_____

_____

_____

_____

_____

SEASONS

*"God blesses you who are hungry now,
for you will be satisfied.
God blesses you who weep now,
for in due time you will laugh."*

LUKE 6:21 NLT

Do you ever find yourself wishing that one season would end so that you could go into the next one? Maybe you are waiting for summer when you can go outside and spend a lot of time in the sun and water. You could be waiting for fall because that is when your sports team starts games again. You might even be waiting for winter so that you can play in the snow.

It's good to know that cool things happen in every season. God says that however you feel, there will be a time when those feelings come to an end, and you will be blessed with different feelings. It's good to be thankful for each season you are in. Being thankful helps us focus on the positive things about the different seasons instead of the negative things. It says to God that you trust him to work in every situation, and he loves it when we ask him to do that!

God, I am thankful that you created all the different seasons—both physical seasons and life seasons. Help me to remember that there are good times to be found in each season. I want to be grateful at all times and trust you to do a wonderful work in me.

DID YOU KNOW...

There is something good about every season!

In the spring, there is more fresh produce to eat, we can finally let fresh air into the house, and the beauty of nature is visible all around us.

In the summer, we tend to spend more time with family and friends, and we do more activities outside which helps reduce stress and puts us in a better mood.

During the fall, cool air creates a better sleeping environment, and changing colors make you feel more relaxed. The cold and cloudy weather actually helps your brain work better!

In winter, we are usually forced to stop and rest. Allergies clear up and our immune system is boosted. Our bodies also burn more calories trying to keep us warm.

Thank God that he has given us these different seasons to enjoy and to benefit from.

Act of Gratitude

I am thankful to God for different seasons.

Here's what I am going to do this week
to show how grateful I am.

_____

_____

_____

_____

_____

_____

_____

_____

_____

_____

GOOD GIFTS

*Every good action and perfect gift is from God.
These good gifts come down from the Creator
of the sun, moon, and stars.*

JAMES 1:17 NCV

Do you look forward to celebrating your birthday?
A lot of children can hardly sleep the night before
Christmas. Sometimes waiting to open gifts is hard!
When we finally rip that paper off the box to see
what's inside, are we always happy? Sometimes
what's inside the box is exactly what we hoped for.
Other times we are met with a surprise that doesn't
seem so wonderful.

Do you know that our heavenly Father loves to
give us gifts? What's even better is that all of his
gifts are good. God knows us better than anyone
else does, and because of this he knows exactly
what we need and when we need it. Thank God
now for the perfect gifts he has given you.

God, you have been so good to me. You know what I need better than anyone else does. You even know what I want. Thank you that you are such a good Father that you give what is perfect for me every time you give me a gift. Help me to be grateful for all that you have blessed me with. I want to see the goodness in every one of your gifts.

IN THE GIFT BOX BELOW, WRITE A LIST OF GIFTS GOD HAS BLESSED YOU WITH RECENTLY. REMEMBER TO THANK HIM FOR EACH ONE THIS WEEK.

Act of Gratitude

I am thankful to God for his good and perfect gifts.

Here's what I am going to do this week
to show how grateful I am.

_____

_____

_____

_____

_____

_____

_____

_____

_____

FURRY FRIENDS

The Lord God had formed all the wild animals and all the birds in the sky. He had made all of them out of the ground. He brought them to the man to see what names he would give them. And the name the man gave each living creature became its name.

GENESIS 2:19 NIRV

Do you like animals? Do you have a pet? What name did you give your pet, or what name would you like to give a pet if you had one? Did you know that God let Adam name all of the animals in the world? That's a lot of names to come up with!

God made animals for us to take care of, and for us to enjoy. God also made animals to help us. Our furry friends can be a good place to go for a comforting hug or a listening ear. They are always happy to see us, they keep us company when we feel lonely, and they can make us laugh when they do silly things. Thank God for the furry friends in your life today.

God, you have created so many wonderful animals for us to enjoy. Thank you for the monkeys in the zoo that make us laugh, the dogs at home that keep us company, and the birds in the trees that sing beautiful songs. I am so grateful for my furry friends!

CREATE AN ANIMAL IN THE SPACE BELOW.
GIVE IT A NEW NAME AND SAY WHAT IT IS BEST AT.
THEN IMAGINE HOW MUCH FUN GOD MUST HAVE HAD
WHEN HE CREATED ALL THE ANIMALS IN THE WORLD.

Act of Gratitude

I am thankful to God for my furry friends.

Here's what I am going to do this week
to show how grateful I am.

_____

_____

_____

_____

_____

_____

_____

_____

_____

A WALL OF PRAISE

*You have made sure that children
and infants praise you.
Their praise is a wall
that stops the talk of your enemies.*

PSALM 8:2 NIRV

Some people say it's the little things that matter,
but they aren't always talking about things that are
small in size. There are things that happen every
day without us even thinking about them. These
things might seem small, but they are actually very
important. Like hearts beating or bees making
honey.

Sometimes children notice things that grown-ups
don't really pay attention to anymore. They stop to
smell the flowers, and watch the ants collect food.
They praise God for the sun and the moon and
the trees. You are precious to God, and he loves
it when you thank him for the wonderful things he
has created.

God, thank you for everything you have created. Help me to remember the small things too. Things that maybe other people don't see. I want to be aware of all the beauty and wonder around me. Thank you that you love to listen to me. You love it when I shout your praises.

STOP TO SMELL THE FLOWERS IN THIS GRID GAME.

Draw a line from beginning to end that passes through every box with a flower in it once. The line can go up, down, left, or right, but not diagonally.

Act of Gratitude

I am thankful to God for all the small things.

Here's what I am going to do this week
to show how grateful I am.

_____

_____

_____

_____

_____

_____

_____

_____

_____

HE KNOWS

My God will meet all your needs. He will meet them in keeping with his wonderful riches. These riches come to you because you belong to Christ Jesus.

PHILIPPIANS 4:19 NIRV

Do you ever worry about where you will live or where your next meal will come from? Most children don't have to think about those things, but some do. It is comforting to know that God will make sure you have everything you need.

God has blessed us with so much. And sometimes, he gives us things before we even ask or before the thought enters our minds. Thank God for knowing exactly what you need when you need it, and for providing it happily.

God, I can't even begin to imagine how you know everything about me. You know what I need and what I want. You delight in providing for me. Help me to keep an attitude of thankfulness for all that you give to me.

FIGURE OUT THE SECRET MESSAGE BY USING THE CODE BELOW:

◎	▲	☼	□	◆	✓	❖	◆	❀	✝	☺	✐	≈
A	B	C	D	E	F	G	H	I	J	K	L	M

★	↑	↓	●	⌘	❁	✖	⁂	◙	✳	✂	×	❄
N	O	P	Q	R	S	T	U	V	W	X	Y	Z

※↑⁂⌘ ✓◎✖◆◆⌘ ☺★↑✳❁

◆✂◎☼✖✐✂ ✳◆◎✖ ※↑⁂ ★◆◆□

◆◙◆★ ▲◆✓↑⌘◆ ※↑⁂ ◎❀☺ ◆❀≈

≈◎✖✖◆◆✳ 6:8

Act of Gratitude

I am thankful to God for knowing what I need.

Here's what I am going to do this week
to show how grateful I am.

_____

_____

_____

_____

_____

_____

_____

_____

_____

FAMILY

Then the Lord God said,
"It is not good for the man to be alone.
I will make a helper who is right for him."
GENESIS 2:18 NCV

Families are a very important part of our lives. They are all different and special. God placed you in your family for a reason. He gave you the people you live with to love you and to help you. And he put you there to love and help them too.

You might look like other people in your family, or you might look totally different. You may be interested in music and they are interested in sports. The most important thing is that you all love and help each other.

God, thank you for placing me in my family. I am so grateful for them even though we are sometimes very different. I know you put me here for a special reason—to love and to be loved. Help me to show my gratitude to the people who are so close to me. I want them to know how much I love them, and how grateful I am for their help.

EVEN IN FAMILIES WHERE SIBLINGS LOOK VERY SIMILAR, THERE IS ALWAYS SOMETHING UNIQUE ABOUT EVERY INDIVIDUAL. CAN YOU FIGURE OUT WHICH TWO PICTURES ARE EXACTLY THE SAME?

Act of Gratitude

I am thankful to God for my family.

Here's what I am going to do this week
to show how grateful I am.

_____

_____

_____

_____

_____

_____

_____

_____

_____

FRIENDSHIP

A friend loves at all times.
PROVERBS 17:17 ESV

Friends are a very important part of our lives. Some friends we keep for many years, and others we have for only a short time. Making friends is easy for some people but it's hard for others. When you find someone who shares a lot of the same values as you do, you should hold on to them and try to grow your friendship.

Friends play together, talk about life together, laugh together, and cry together. When we truly love our friends, we choose to believe the best about them, and we work to make the friendship last. God gave us a huge gift when he gave us friends. We should remember to thank him for that daily!

God, thank you for my friends. I am so grateful for them even though we don't always see things the same way. I know you put them in my life for a good reason, and I want to keep them close to me in whatever ways I can. Help me to show them how much I love them and how thankful I am that they are my friends.

FIND YOUR FRIEND AT THE CENTER OF THIS MAZE.

Start
here

Act of Gratitude

I am thankful to God for my friends.

Here's what I am going to do this week
to show how grateful I am.

_____

_____

_____

_____

_____

_____

_____

_____

_____

NEVER ALONE

I can never escape from your Spirit!
I can never get away from your presence!
If I go up to heaven, you are there;
if I go down to the grave, you are there.
If I ride the wings of the morning,
if I dwell by the farthest oceans,
even there your hand will guide me,
and your strength will support me.

PSALM 139:7-10 NLT

Isn't this verse wonderful? God says in his Word that he will never leave us. No matter where we go, we cannot be alone. When we are afraid, he is with us. When we don't know what to do, he is with us. When we are sad, he is with us. And in our happy moments, he is there too!

There is no getting away from God, so don't even try. Delight in his nearness and thank him for staying close by your side. Ask him for help whenever you need it, and share your special moments with him too. He loves to hear from you.

God, thank you that you are always close to me. When I am sad, afraid, or lonely, help me to remember that I can talk to you because you are near. When I have something to celebrate, remind me to share that with you too because you love to celebrate with me! You care about every detail of my life. I am so grateful that you are always close.

DID YOU KNOW?

In order to speak a sentence, about 100 muscles in the chest, neck, jaw, tongue, and lips have to work together. The first six months of life are the most important for a child to develop language skills. By the age of six, many children can say about 2,600 words, but they actually understand closer to 20,000 words.

God understands every word you know—so go ahead and share everything that's on your heart!

Act of Gratitude

I am thankful to God for always being close to me.

Here's what I am going to do this week
to show how grateful I am.

_____

_____

_____

_____

_____

_____

_____

_____

_____

SPECIAL GIFTS

In his grace, God has given us different gifts for doing certain things well. So if God has given you the ability to prophesy, speak out with as much faith as God has given you. If your gift is serving others, serve them well. If you are a teacher, teach well. If your gift is to encourage others, be encouraging. If it is giving, give generously. If God has given you leadership ability, take the responsibility seriously. And if you have a gift for showing kindness to others, do it gladly.

ROMANS 12:6-8 NLT

What do you really like to do? Maybe you take food orders from your parents so you can serve them breakfast in bed, or perhaps you find yourself setting up a classroom to teach your stuffed animals or siblings. Maybe you're the kind of person who always has something nice to say to someone else, or you give away your toys without thinking twice.

God has created us all with special gifts. Things that come naturally to us can be a good indicator of what our gifts are. If you don't know what your gift is, ask some of the people in your life who know you best. Thank God for giving you a special gift and begin using it for him today!

God, thank you that you have given me a special gift. I want to use what you have given me to bless others and to make your name known. I want people to feel your love and to know your joy through me sharing my gift. Help me to listen to you and to be bold.

UNSCRAMBLE THE LETTERS TO REVEAL SOME OF THE SPECIAL GIFTS GOD GIVES TO US.

DLPSIEARHE _ _ _ _ _ _ _ _ _ _

EPYOCHRP _ _ _ _ _ _ _ _

IVGGNI _ _ _ _ _ _

DSKENISN _ _ _ _ _ _ _ _

REOTMCUGENEA _ _ _ _ _ _ _ _ _ _ _ _

NSEIVRG _ _ _ _ _ _ _

GTAHEICN _ _ _ _ _ _ _ _

Act of Gratitude

I am thankful to God for giving me a special gift.

Here's what I am going to do this week
to show how grateful I am.

_____

_____

_____

_____

_____

_____

_____

_____

_____

BEAUTY OF CREATION

Ever since the world was created, people have seen the earth and sky. Through everything God made, they can clearly see his invisible qualities—his eternal power and divine nature. So they have no excuse for not knowing God.

ROMANS 1:20 NLT

There is beauty all around us. Just take a look outside. Whether the skies are blue or filled with clouds, we can marvel at how everything was formed. Trees stand tall with branches reaching to the sky, flowers bloom with beautiful fragrance, and animals scamper through forests and into burrows.

Do you ever take a moment to thank God for his amazing creation? The Bible tells us that the world is full of examples that prove God is real. If you haven't done it already, start looking for the beauty in God's world and thank him for it.

God, thank you for the beauty of creation. You have made so many amazing things and I can't help but stand in wonder. Help me to pay attention to the beauty around me and to point it out to others, so they will also see how great you are.

Starting with the letter I, write a letter, skip three, and then write the next letter.

Start here
↓

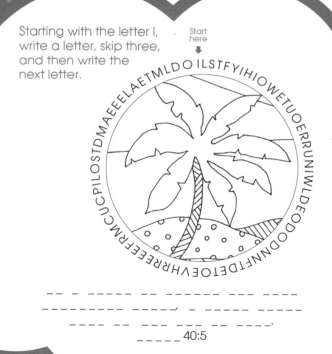

__ _ _____ __ _____ ___ ____
_____ ____' _ _____ _____
____ __ ___ ___ __ ___.
_____ 40:5

Act of Gratitude

I am thankful to God for the beauty of his creation.

Here's what I am going to do this week
to show how grateful I am.

_____

_____

_____

_____

_____

_____

_____

_____

THE HUMAN BRAIN

I will give thanks to You,
for I am fearfully and wonderfully made;
Wonderful are Your works,
And my soul knows it very well.

PSALM 139:14 NASB

The human brain is incredible. It causes our bodies to work in ways that we don't even have to think about. It stores information that helps us make it through life. It allows us to learn new things and communicate with others.

Sometimes you might have difficulty understanding something. A really good way to engage your brain in these situations is to ask questions. Ask your parents, teachers, and siblings, or ask God! Can you stop and thank God for your brain right now?

God, thank you creating me fearfully and wonderfully. My brain has so many incredible qualities and abilities. Help me to remember to fill my brain with the right kind of knowledge— your Word!

DID YOU KNOW?

The brain is the most complicated organ in the human body. It is made up of about 75% water and uses 20% of the oxygen and blood in the body. It has about one hundred billion neurons in it. Information has to run between the neurons in order for us to be able to think, see, or do. Information can pass between neurons at speeds of up to 250 miles per hour!

Act of Gratitude

I am thankful to God for my brain.

Here's what I am going to do this week
to show how grateful I am.

_____

_____

_____

_____

_____

_____

_____

_____

_____

FORGIVENESS

He has removed our sins as far from us
as the east is from the west.

PSALM 103:12 NLT

Have you ever messed something up when you were writing? What did you do? Sometimes even after you erase a mistake, you can still see faint lines on the paper where the mistake was made. Or maybe you were using a pen and you had to try another way to cover up the error—but you still know where the mistake was made.

When we sin, sometimes we think about it over and over again. We remind ourselves of how bad we were and continue to feel ashamed. God's forgiveness works better than an eraser. When we tell him we're sorry for our sin, he takes it away and cleans it up so we don't have to keep remembering it. Trust that God has forgiven you today and choose to forgive your own mistakes as well.

Thank you, God, for your forgiveness that washes me clean and helps me start new. I don't want to keep remembering the mistakes I've made and sins I've committed. I want to walk in your forgiveness and make wise decisions going forward.

CAN YOU TELL WHAT HAS BEEN ERASED FROM THE BOTTOM PICTURE? CIRCLE THE 10 THINGS THAT ARE MISSING.

Act of Gratitude

I am thankful to God for his forgiveness of sins.

Here's what I am going to do this week
to show how grateful I am.

_____

_____

_____

_____

_____

_____

_____

_____

_____

EDUCATION

*Remember what you are taught,
and listen carefully to words of knowledge.*
PROVERBS 23:12 NCV

You might not like having to go to school or doing
school work at home. But do you know that getting
an education is actually a privilege? There are
many children around the world who don't get the
opportunity to learn how to read and write.

We learn some pretty important things at school
that help us when we grow up. The Bible tells us to
listen carefully to wisdom. Whether your teacher
is at public school, private school, or home, they
have a lot of wisdom to share with you. So listen
carefully, and don't waste the opportunity to learn
new things.

God, I am thankful for the ability to learn. You have given me the privilege of getting an education and I don't want to take it for granted. Help me to apply myself to my studies and to thank my teachers for their wisdom and time.

DID YOU KNOW?

There are over 780 million adults in the world today who cannot read or write. When people don't have an opportunity to learn, they are more likely to live a poor lifestyle with many different types of difficulties. In poorer countries, almost 45% of children between the ages of 6-11 do not attend school.

Act of Gratitude

I am thankful to God for the gift of education.

Here's what I am going to do this week
to show how grateful I am.

_____

_____

_____

_____

_____

_____

_____

_____

_____

_____

DAY OF REST

"Here is a place of rest;
let the weary rest here.
This is a place of quiet rest."
ISAIAH 28:12 NLT

Sundays are typically the day that families attend church. As the sun comes up, we climb out of bed, get dressed, eat breakfast, and head to church to worship the one true God. It's good to set aside a day to rest. Instead of doing what we do every other day, Sundays can be a good day for focusing on relationship—with God, family, and friends.

There's really no better way to start a day than by praising God with a bunch of other people. Thank God today for encouraging you to take a break from your usual activities one day out of seven. He knows you better than anyone else, and he understands the importance of rest.

Thank you, God, for encouraging me to rest. I know I need to spend a day each week focusing on building relationship with you and the other people you have put in my life. Help me to slow down and see the importance of building relationship and taking a break from the usual busyness of life.

DID YOU KNOW?

Resting helps your memory, metabolism, mood, heart health, and immune system. There are different types of rest: sensory, emotional, mental, and physical.

Sensory rest is when you give your senses a break. Close your eyes for a couple minutes after watching a screen for an hour.

Emotional rest is when you create space or balance in feelings. Don't let yourself get too worked up about someone else's problems.

Mental rest is when you stop your mind from overthinking. Don't think about too many things at once.

Physical rest is when you let your body relax. Take a nap when you feel tired or get good sleep at night.

Act of Gratitude

I am thankful to God for a day of rest.

Here's what I am going to do this week
to show how grateful I am.

_____

_____

_____

_____

_____

_____

_____

_____

_____

HEALTHY CHOICES

You should know that your body is a temple for the Holy Spirit who is in you. You have received the Holy Spirit from God. So you do not belong to yourselves, because you were bought by God for a price. So honor God with your bodies.

1 CORINTHIANS 6:19-20 NCV

God created our bodies for life in this world. Bodies can get sick or hurt, so we need to take care of them. One way we can do that is to be careful what we eat. God gave us many healthy foods to eat. He filled the Garden of Eden with plants that grew fruit and vegetables with so many different colors and textures. Some are soft and juicy, others are hard and crunchy. We sometimes eat the outer layer and other times we don't.

The foods God gave us are full of vitamins and minerals that our bodies need to work properly and to fight off sickness. We get strong bones and muscles when we eat good food. When we think of our bodies as temples for the Holy Spirit, it should make us want to eat healthy foods. Ask God to help you make good choices for a healthy body today!

God, thank you for creating my body. Help me to make healthy choices when it comes to what I am putting in it. You have given me so many good fruits and vegetables to eat that have the vitamins and minerals I need to grow strong bones and muscles. I want to honor you with the body you have given me.

DID YOU KNOW?

These vitamins and minerals are found in many fruits and vegetables:

Vitamin A – for your eyes and skin

Vitamin C – for fighting disease

Calcium – for healthy bones and teeth

Fiber – for heart health

Iron – for blood and cells

Magnesium – for muscles

Potassium – for blood pressure

Act of Gratitude

I am thankful to God for healthy choices.

Here's what I am going to do this week
to show how grateful I am.

_____

_____

_____

_____

_____

_____

_____

_____

_____

SUNSHINE

God said, "Let there be light." And there was light.
God saw that the light was good.
He separated the light from the darkness.
GENESIS 1:3-4 NIRV

A little sunshine goes a long way to make a day better. It gives us light and warms the earth. We often feel happier when the sun is shining. We can play outside without having to wear a jacket! On hot days, we can have fun in the water: swimming in a pool, running through the sprinklers, playing with water balloons, or shooting soaker sprayers. Sunny days are also good for picnics, playing at the park, and grilling on the deck.

Being outside on a sunny day, enjoying the fresh air, having fun, and spending time with the people we love is good for our hearts, minds, and bodies. We should remember to thank God for the sunshine and all that it allows us to do.

God, thank you for the sun. When it is shining in the sky, everything feels lighter and brighter. I am so grateful for all the things I can do when the sun is out. Help me not to complain about the weather. Instead, I want to focus on being grateful when the sun is out and taking advantage of those beautiful days.

```
                  A
   E              O                    O
     P            V              S
       J    E P A E K    U
         C G R C P R N
       H L O E A O S C C
       C O O S T H E L P
Y O J A U D E I W I N D O W D
       E D N N O E C B R
       B S E C N V G A M
         M S E T G O N
       R   S A R S A    A
   A              U              H
 W                S              C
                  T
```

FIND THESE WORDS

BEACH
CHANGE
CLOUDS
GOODNESS
HELP

HOPE
JOY
PRESENCE
SOAR

SUNSHINE
TRUST
VACATION
WARM
WINDOW

Act of Gratitude

I am thankful to God for the sunshine.

Here's what I am going to do this week
to show how grateful I am.

_____

_____

_____

_____

_____

_____

_____

_____

_____

LAUGHTER

Our mouths were filled with laughter.
Our tongues sang with joy.
Then the people of other nations said,
"The Lord has done great things for them."
PSALM 126:2 NIRV

Do you think Adam laughed when he first saw an ostrich? Maybe Eve cracked up when she heard the name of the Dodo bird. God must like to laugh too. He created some pretty funny things.

Laughing can help pull us out of a grumpy mood and put a smile back on our faces. We can laugh with others when we see, hear, or say funny things. Do you make silly faces or tell jokes to make the people around you laugh? That is a blessing! Thank God for the gift of laughter today.

I am so grateful for laughter, God. When I'm laughing with other people, life just feels so much fuller. Thank you for making funny things, and for giving us a sense of humor. It's exciting to think that you laugh sometimes too. It makes me want to enjoy life even more than I already do. You are truly a good God!

HERE ARE A FEW JOKES TO GET YOU LAUGHING.

Who was the greatest female businessperson in the Bible?

Pharaoh's daughter. She went down to the bank of the Nile and drew out a little prophet.

At what time of day was Adam created?

A little before Eve.

Why couldn't they have apples on Noah's Ark?

Because everything was in pears.

Act of Gratitude

I am thankful to God for the gift of laughter.

Here's what I am going to do this week
to show how grateful I am.

_____

_____

_____

_____

_____

_____

_____

_____

_____

MY HOUSE

By wisdom a house is built.
Through understanding it is made secure.
Through knowledge its rooms are filled
with priceless and beautiful things.

PROVERBS 24:3-4 NIRV

Think for a moment about your house. What does it look like? Do you constantly compare your house to other people's houses? Are you bothered that you don't have your own room? Or that the furniture is old? Is the bathroom too small?

If you have a roof over your head, and a bed to sleep in, you should be very grateful! Many people around the world do not have either of those. The most important thing about a house is that your family is there. God has blessed you with a place to call home. You can choose to be thankful for your house no matter what it looks like.

God, thank you for my house. Thank you for all that is in it, including my family. You have blessed me with a roof over my head and a bed to sleep in, and I know that is more than what a lot of people have. Help me to have an attitude of gratitude when I think about my house instead of complaining about how it could be better.

DRAW A PICTURE OF YOUR HOUSE HERE AND THEN REMEMBER TO THANK GOD FOR A WONDERFUL PLACE TO EAT, SLEEP, AND ENJOY TIME WITH YOUR FAMILY!

Act of Gratitude

I am thankful to God for my house.

Here's what I am going to do this week
to show how grateful I am.

_____

_____

_____

_____

_____

_____

_____

_____

_____

_____

PROTECTION

Let all those who go to you for safety be glad.
Let them always sing for joy.
Spread your cover over them and keep them safe.
Then those who love you will be glad
because of you.

When you have a bad dream, what do you do? When you are afraid, who do you talk to? Did you know that King David in the Bible had a lot of scary moments? Sometimes he even feared for his life! Whenever David was afraid, he went to God for protection and safety. You can do the same thing!

When you are a child of God, you can count on him to keep you safe. This doesn't mean that you will never feel afraid, or that you won't ever hurt yourself. It means that you can trust that God knows what is best for you and that he is watching out for you. He will pick you up when you fall, and he will cover you with his blanket of safety when you run to him.

God, thank you for being my safe place. You are always ready to protect me. Thank you for your steady arms that pick me up when I fall, and for your blanket of comfort that is ready for me when I am afraid. I trust you with all that I have and all that I am.

Find your way through the wall of protection!

Start here

You made it!

Act of Gratitude

I am thankful to God for protecting me.

Here's what I am going to do this week
to show how grateful I am.

_____

_____

_____

_____

_____

_____

_____

_____

_____

RUNNING WATER

*"Anyone who drinks the water I give them
will never be thirsty. In fact, the water I give them
will become a spring of water in them.
It will flow up into eternal life."*

JOHN 4:14 NIRV

Jesus knew the importance of water. We need water to survive. Whether we are drinking it, cooking with it, or using it to wash something, water is critical to our survival. In many places around the world, there is very little running water. Sometimes the only water available is dirty water.

Have you ever had the main water supply shut off in your house for an hour or more? How many times did you try to run water in that short amount of time? It's easy to complain about the water taking too long to heat up or running out of hot water altogether. It's easy to be picky about what our water tastes like. It's time to stop complaining and be grateful for the water that we can get so easily.

God, thank you for the gift of water. I am so blessed to be able to go to the faucet and fill my cup with water for a refreshing drink, or fill the sink with hot water to wash dishes, or fill a pot to cook food on the stove. Help me to continue to be grateful for the gift of clean running water.

DID YOU KNOW?

More than one billion people have to travel 15 minutes to get to a safe water source. About 423 million people around the world get their water from unprotected wells and springs. This means the water they are drinking may not be safe. 159 million people collect their water from lakes, ponds, rivers, and streams which likely contain diseases.

Act of Gratitude

I am thankful to God for the gift of water.

Here's what I am going to do this week
to show how grateful I am.

_____

_____

_____

_____

_____

_____

_____

_____

_____

GROWN-UPS

*"Honor your father and mother,
just as the Lord your God has commanded you.
Then you will live a long time in the land he is giving
you. And things will go well with you there."*

DEUTERONOMY 5:16 NIRV

The older people in our life are placed there for a
reason. We need help. Sometimes it's hard to obey
our parents. We might not want to do what they
are asking us to do. We might not like what they are
saying. But most parents are trying their best to do
what is right—and most of the time, they are asking
us to do things that are good for us.

One of the ten commandments is to honor your
parents. It's the only commandment with a promise
attached: honor your parents and it will go well
with you. Instead of arguing about how your way
is better, or complaining about what you are
being asked to do, honor your parents through
obedience. You might be surprised how your
attitude changes.

God, thank you for the people in my life who take care of me. I don't always like what they ask me to do, but I know that they are trying to help me be a better person. Help me to honor my parents and others in authority over me. I want to do what is right before you.

CREATE A FAMILY TREE AND THEN PRAY FOR THOSE WHO ARE LISTED ON IT!

Act of Gratitude

I am thankful to God for my parents.

Here's what I am going to do this week
to show how grateful I am.

_____

_____

_____

_____

_____

_____

_____

_____

_____

VACATION TIME

*"Come with me by yourselves to a quiet place.
You need to get some rest."*
MARK 6:31 NIRV

What is your idea of a dream vacation? Do you like warm beaches, snow-capped mountains, cabins by the lake, foreign cities? It's great to get away from home and enjoy the world that God created. When we go on vacation, we tend to slow down, spend time together, try new things, and... rest.

Even Jesus needed to get away to a quiet place and rest. He encouraged his disciples to do the same. When we are busy every day with different tasks and activities, we often forget to take time to rest. The next time you get to go on vacation somewhere, thank God for the opportunity to relax and enjoy his creation.

God, thank you for time away from the busyness of life. Thank you for giving me an opportunity to rest and relax. I am so grateful for all that you have created for us to enjoy. Help me not to take my vacation time for granted, or to waste it doing things that are not restful.

UNSCRAMBLE THE LETTERS BELOW TO DISCOVER POPULAR VACATION SPOTS.

RIPSA _ _ _ _ _

WNE RYOK _ _ _ _ _ _ _

NDOLNO _ _ _ _ _ _

IJIBGNE _ _ _ _ _ _ _

UHLOONUL _ _ _ _ _ _ _ _

IBOINRA _ _ _ _ _ _ _

DYSENY _ _ _ _ _ _

ANS RCSIFONAC _ _ _ _ _ _ _ _ _ _ _

Act of Gratitude

I am thankful to God for vacation time.

Here's what I am going to do this week
to show how grateful I am.

_____

_____

_____

_____

_____

_____

_____

_____

_____

MY SENSES

"Blessed are your eyes because they see.
And blessed are your ears because they hear."
MATTHEW 13:16 NIRV

Can you list the five senses? *Sight, sound, smell, touch, and taste.* Do you ever think about how much you use each of these senses every day? Do you wake up to birds chirping, or someone lightly stroking your face? Do you see the clothes you will soon put on? Can you smell breakfast cooking in the kitchen? Are you excited about tasting pancakes, eggs, or bacon?

God has given us the wonderful blessing of senses. Some of our senses may be stronger than others, but we can thank God for all of them anyway. When we get to heaven, our senses will be made whole and we will see, hear, smell, touch, and taste without limitation. What an amazing experience that will be!

God, thank you for giving me the pleasure of senses. You created the ability to see, hear, taste, touch, and smell for my delight. Thank you that one day I will have all of my senses working to perfection. Right now, though, I am grateful for what I do have. Help me to pay attention to my senses and to remember to thank you for them often.

DID YOU KNOW...

Our senses are amazing! Here are some fun facts about the five senses.

Our eyes can process 36,000 pieces of information in an hour. They are responsible for 85% of our knowledge.

Our noses can smell about 10,000 different odors. About 80% of what we taste is related to our sense of smell.

We can't taste what our saliva can't dissolve. If you were to dry out your mouth and put something dry (like sugar) on your tongue, you wouldn't be able to taste it.

Our sense of hearing depends on tiny hairs deep inside our ears. If we lose those hairs, we lose our hearing.

Touch is extremely important for the healthy development of babies.

Act of Gratitude

I am thankful to God for my senses.

Here's what I am going to do this week
to show how grateful I am.

_____

_____

_____

_____

_____

_____

_____

_____

_____

BEAUTIFUL DIFFERENCES

"I will give it to you.
I will give you a wise and understanding heart.
So here is what will be true of you.
There has never been anyone like you.
And there never will be."

1 KINGS 3:12 NIRV

Can you imagine how boring the world would be if we were all the same? What if we looked the same, thought the same, felt the same, and acted the same. What a terrible shame that would be!

God has created us to look, feel, think, and act differently. When we embrace our differences and learn to work together, beautiful things can happen. God wants us to love each other unconditionally and to show the world his love in this way. The next time you notice someone is very different than you are, thank God for his wisdom in making each of you unique, and choose to love your differences!

God, thank you for making us all so different. Help me to see differences as being positive instead of negative. I want to work well with others and learn how to use our differences to do amazing things together for you.

SPOT THE DIFFERENCES

Pick out all the things that makes these twins unique.

Act of Gratitude

I am thankful to God for making us all different.

Here's what I am going to do this week
to show how grateful I am.

_____

_____

_____

_____

_____

_____

_____

_____

_____

_____

MODERN MEDICINE

Jesus went everywhere in Galilee, teaching in the synagogues, preaching the Good News about the kingdom of heaven, and healing all the people's diseases and sicknesses.

MATTHEW 4:23 NCV

When Jesus walked the earth he performed many miracles—healing the sick and providing things that people needed. Sometimes we see healing from miracles like this today, and other times healing comes in the form of medicine.

God has given us incredible brains. There are people all over the world researching cures for different diseases. They are discovering and developing many kinds of medicines that can help us when we are sick. Thank God today for his gift of healing and for the wisdom he is granting to researchers and doctors!

God, I know you don't like us to feel sick. It was your desire from the beginning that we would never experience sickness or death. Thank you for allowing us to develop medicines and cures that help relieve some of the pain and sickness in the world today. I look forward to the day when there will be no more need for medicine because we will all be completely healthy!

DID YOU KNOW?

In 1928, Alexander Fleming discovered an antibiotic completely by accident. When he was cleaning out his lab, he noticed that mold had formed in one of the petri dishes and it had killed the bacteria in that dish! With a little more research on how to recreate that mold, penicillin was born. This is one of the greatest medical discoveries of all time.

Act of Gratitude

I am thankful to God for modern medicine.

Here's what I am going to do this week
to show how grateful I am.

_____

_____

_____

_____

_____

_____

_____

_____

_____

SYMPHONY OF WONDER

Speak to each other with psalms, hymns, and spiritual songs, singing and making music in your hearts to the Lord.

EPHESIANS 5:19 NCV

Have you ever watched a movie without sound? How did you feel? Music is used in movies to help capture emotion—building tension or excitement, and causing the audience to engage in the feelings of the characters.

Music is a really good way for us to express our gratitude and thanksgiving to God. He tells us in his Word to sing new songs and to create music for him. When we put our emotions to music, it is a beautiful offering to God, and it blesses others as well. Be encouraged by the gift of music today. Join creation in the symphony of wonder before God.

God, thank you so much for the gift of music. I am so grateful for voices and instruments that blend together to create beautiful sounds. You have blessed so many people with musical talent that can be used to worship you and encourage others. Help me to engage in worshiping you with all of my talents as well.

DID YOU KNOW?

Music is one of very few activities that uses your whole brain. It can engage the emotional, motor, and creative areas of the brain at the same time. Music has been linked to better learning, workout performance, and emotional connection.

Spending time listening to (or playing) worship music is a great way for you to connect with God. Try it this week!

Act of Gratitude

I am thankful to God for the gift of music.

Here's what I am going to do this week
to show how grateful I am.

_____

_____

_____

_____

_____

_____

_____

_____

_____

WHAT TO WEAR

"Why do you worry about clothes? Look at how the lilies in the field grow. They don't work or make clothes for themselves. But I tell you that even Solomon with his riches was not dressed as beautifully as one of these flowers."

EPHESIANS 5:19 NCV

Do you sometimes get stuck in the trap of comparing your clothes with others? When you see someone wearing something you really like, does it bother you that you don't have something similar? Look at what Jesus said about clothes. We don't need to worry. God will provide for us. He will give us what we need.

It's easy to fall into the trap of placing too much importance on the clothes we wear. The world will tell you what is cool and what isn't. People won't always like your outfit. It really doesn't matter. God is your provider and it says in this verse that he clothes the lilies in the field in better clothing than the richest king in history. So trust God to provide what's right for you, and be thankful when he does!

Thank you, God, for providing for me. You have given me clothes to wear—probably more clothes than I even really need. Help me to remember that I don't need to worry about the kind of clothes I have. I choose to be content with what you have given me.

DID YOU KNOW?

The two main reasons for clothing are for warmth and protection, but there are other factors that help people decide what to wear too. Some jobs or schools require uniforms. This means you wear similar clothes to everyone around you—it's a way of identifying who you are with. Do you watch sports? Does your team have a uniform? A lot of people will buy clothes that look like their favorite team's uniform to show that they support that team. Not too long ago, most clothes were made at home. Today they are made much more cheaply and quickly in large factories.

Act of Gratitude

I am thankful to God for my clothes.

Here's what I am going to do this week
to show how grateful I am.

_____

_____

_____

_____

_____

_____

_____

_____

_____

SURPRISE!

*You have done amazing things
we did not expect.
You came down, and the mountains
trembled before you.*

ISAIAH 64:3 NCV

"Surprise!" Maybe you got a puppy for Christmas, or someone you love showed up at your door after being gone for a long time, or your dad came home and told the family you were all going out for dinner. When wonderful things happen that you had no idea about, you can thank God for his gift of surprises.

We cannot possibly know all that God is going to bless us with in this life, but we can choose to thank him when he surprises us with his good gifts. The next time you are blown away by something unexpected and amazing, remember to turn your attention to God and show him your appreciation.

God, thank you for great surprises that show me how much you love me. You are the giver of good gifts and you have blessed me with so much. Help me to remember to show gratitude and appreciation when I am amazed once again by something you have done for me.

Write about your biggest surprise!

Act of Gratitude

I am thankful to God for surprises.

Here's what I am going to do this week
to show how grateful I am.

_____

_____

_____

_____

_____

_____

_____

_____

_____

_____

_____

NEW MERCIES

The LORD's love never ends;
his mercies never stop.
They are new every morning;
LORD, your loyalty is great.
LAMENTATIONS 3:22-23 NCV

At the end of a rough day, it's easy to feel discouraged. Life is hard and hope may even seem lost. You might have tried all day to do the right thing, but somehow you kept making unwise choices. Do you know that God gives you new mercy every day?

Do you know what mercy is? Mercy is compassion where it's not deserved. It's favor where there shouldn't be any. When you make mistakes and then admit them to God, he wipes them off the screen—never to be seen again. And you wake up to a new day, with new mercy for that day and love that never quits.

God, thank you for your amazing love and new mercy for each day. It's hard to make the right decisions all the time, and I know I don't always make great choices. Help me to confess my sin and weakness to you and to hold on to your mercy every morning.

USE THE CODE BELOW TO FIGURE OUT THE SECRET MESSAGE.

◎	⋏	☼	▢	◗	✓	❖	◆	❀	✝	☺	✐	〰
A	B	C	D	E	F	G	H	I	J	K	L	M

★	↑	↓	●	⌘	❄	✕	❄	▣	✸	✄	✕	❄
N	O	P	Q	R	S	T	U	V	W	X	Y	Z

✕◆◗ ✐↑⌘▢ ❀❀ ❖↑↑▢

THE LORD IS GOOD

✕↑ ◎✐✐; ◗◗ ◗◎❀

TO ALL HE HAS

☼↑〰↓◎❀❀❀↑★ ↑★

COMPASSION ON

◎✐✐ ◗◗ ◗◎❀ 〰◎▢◗.

ALL HE HAS MADE

↓❄◎✐〰 145:9

PSALM 145:9

Act of Gratitude

I am thankful to God for his mercy.

Here's what I am going to do this week
to show how grateful I am.

_____

_____

_____

_____

_____

_____

_____

_____

_____

UNFAILING LOVE

Let your unfailing love surround us, Lord,
for our hope is in you alone.
PSALM 33:22 NLT

Love comes in a lot of different shapes and sizes. Moms and dads love each other in a different way than they love their children. Siblings love each other, but not quite the same as they love their friends. We love food, we love sports, we love art... so what is love really?

The Bible tells us that God is love. It says that love, like God, is patient, kind, and enduring. Love, like God, never fails. The only true definition for love is God himself. We will never be able to find anyone who loves us as well as God does, but we can learn from his example and try to love others like he loves us.

God, you are love. All love begins and ends with you. Thank you for loving me so well. Help me to use your example of love to reach out and love other people. Show me how to best love my family, my friends, my neighbors, and others I don't know very well.

FIND YOUR WAY TO GOD'S HEART!

Start here

Act of Gratitude

I am thankful to God for his love.

Here's what I am going to do this week
to show how grateful I am.

_____

_____

_____

_____

_____

_____

_____

_____

_____

_____

LONG WALKS

Let the skies rejoice and the earth be glad;
let the sea and everything in it shout.
Let the fields and everything in them rejoice.
Then all the trees of the forest will sing for joy.
PSALM 96:11-12 NCV

Picture yourself on a long walk. You look up at the sky and it almost appears happy. Small clouds resemble laughing people and animals at play. As you walk through a field beside the edge of the forest, the wheat stalks are waving. They sound as if they are clapping in the breeze. You enter the forest to find the trees singing. Making your way to the top of the hill, you sit down at a lookout spot. The waves in the ocean below crash against the shore in a continual shout of praise.

You might not find something quite this dramatic every time you go on a walk, but you can bet if you look for the beauty in nature shouting praises back to God, you will find it. Walks are great for your mind, your soul, and your body. The next time you get a chance to go for a long walk, join creation in praising your Maker.

Thank you, God, that all of creation points back to its Creator. You have made this earth and all that surrounds it so beautiful. I cannot even begin to understand how you created everything with such purpose. Not one single detail has been left undone. Help me to praise you the next time I am walking. I want to see your creation with eyes that truly appreciate beauty.

Reveal the secret message!

1. First time around: Write every second letter on the spaces below

2. Second time around: Write the remaining letters on the spaces.

Start here

___ _____ _____ ___ _____
__ ___; ___ _____ _____
___ _____ __ ___ _____.

PSALM 19:1 NIV

Act of Gratitude

I am thankful to God for long walks.

Here's what I am going to do this week
to show how grateful I am.

_____

_____

_____

_____

_____

_____

_____

_____

_____

THE LATEST TECHNOLOGY

Through him all things were made;
without him nothing was made
that has been made.

JOHN 1:3 NIV

You might think God has nothing to do with the latest technology. If you look at this Scripture in John, though, you will see that even the most recent advance in phones, computers, programs, and cars can be attributed to God.

God gave us incredible brains to invent new things. He also gave us the eyes, ears, hands, arms, legs, and feet to carry out the creation of those things. We can video chat with our relatives, take pictures with our phones, and ask our cars how to get somewhere all because God gave us brilliant, creative minds.

Thank you, God, that without you, we would have nothing. Thank you for minds that can ideate and arms and legs that can create. You are not confused by technology no matter how advanced it is. Help me to appreciate people who invent things, but more than that, help me to give you credit where it is due.

USE THE CODE BELOW TO FIGURE OUT THE SECRET MESSAGE.

◎	▲	☼	□	💧	✓	❖	◆	✿	♱	☺	✏	≋
A	B	C	D	E	F	G	H	I	J	K	L	M

★	↑	↓	●	⌘	❀	✖	⁂	▣	✹	✂	✕	❄
N	O	P	Q	R	S	T	U	V	W	X	Y	Z

GREAT IS OUR LORD

AND MIGHTY IN POWER

HIS UNDERSTANDING

HAS NO LIMIT

PSALM 147:5

Act of Gratitude

I am thankful to God for advanced technology.

Here's what I am going to do this week
to show how grateful I am.

_____

_____

_____

_____

_____

_____

_____

_____

_____

HOBBIES

There is nothing better than to enjoy food and drink and to find satisfaction in work. Then I realized that these pleasures are from the hand of God.

Ecclesiastes 2:24 NLT

What is your favorite way to spend time? Maybe you like to draw, color, or paint. Or perhaps you prefer activities like fishing, dancing, or soccer. Reading books, playing games, hiking up a mountain, knitting a sweater... all of these things are considered hobbies. And all of them can be pleasurable activities given to you by God.

King Solomon in all his wisdom realized that God actually wants us to enjoy life. As you swim, sing, sketch, surf, or strum the guitar, direct your attention to God, and thank him for giving you the opportunity to have fun in life.

God, thank you for all the fun things you have given me to do. Help me to remember you as I am enjoying life. Give me wisdom to know when my hobby is becoming too important to me and is taking away from other things that need my attention.

WRITE A LIST OF YOUR TEN FAVORITE THINGS TO DO:

1. _____
2. _____
3. _____
4. _____
5. _____
6. _____
7. _____
8. _____
9. _____
10. _____

Act of Gratitude

I am thankful to God for my hobbies.

Here's what I am going to do this week
to show how grateful I am.

_____

_____

_____

_____

_____

_____

_____

_____

_____

TEAMWORK

He makes the whole body fit together perfectly.
As each part does its own special work,
it helps the other parts grow, so that the whole
body is healthy and growing and full of love.
EPHESIANS 4:16 NLT

God's people are all part of one body. This
Scripture says that God makes the whole body fit
together perfectly, with each part doing its own
special work. The great thing about this is that one
person doesn't have to do everything! The sooner
you can discover what you are really good at,
and what you aren't good at, the better.

When you team up with people who are good at
things you aren't and not good at things you are,
you become a healthy body and you help each
other grow. It's not always easy to get along with
others, especially when you are so different, but it
is rewarding when everyone works together to get
a project done.

God, thank you for the people around me who are good at things that I am not good at. Thank you for giving me special talents that can be shared with others too. I want to be a good teammate and continue to work hard so the body of Christ is made even stronger.

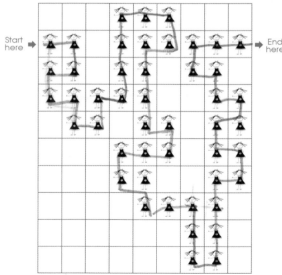

Start here →

End here →

Draw a line from beginning to end that passes through every teammate only once.
The line can go up, down, left, or right, but not diagonally.

Act of Gratitude

I am thankful to God for teamwork.

Here's what I am going to do this week
to show how grateful I am.

_____

_____

_____

_____

_____

_____

_____

_____

_____

EMOTIONS

*Be happy with those who are happy,
and weep with those who weep.*
Romans 12:15 NLT

Emotions are difficult to understand. Sometimes we think it's bad to show our feelings. That's not true. God wants us to let people know how we feel so they can join in our laughter or tears. He wants us to feel compassion for those who seem to have no hope, and extend patience to those who seem to be angry for no reason.

We feel many different emotions in one day. We might go from feeling happy to sad and back to happy in less than five minutes. It's important to understand why specific events cause certain emotions in you. Ask God to help you control your emotions rather than letting them control you.

God, thank you for the different emotions you have created. Help me to be aware of how much my emotions are influencing my decisions. I want to laugh with those who are laughing, and listen to those who need to talk.

DID YOU KNOW?

FOR A LONG TIME, IT HAS BEEN BELIEVED THAT THERE ARE EIGHT BASIC HUMAN EMOTIONS. MORE RECENT STUDIES SAY THERE COULD BE AS MANY AS 27. GIVE EACH EMOTION BELOW A FACE.

JOY   ANGER   SURPRISE   SADNESS

DISGUST   ANTICIPATION   TRUST   FEAR

Act of Gratitude

I am thankful to God for emotions.

Here's what I am going to do this week
to show how grateful I am.

_____

_____

_____

_____

_____

_____

_____

_____

_____

TRANSPORTATION

*"You who ride on white donkeys
and sit on saddle blankets,
and you who walk along the road, listen!"*

JUDGES 5:10 NCV

The way people traveled in Bible times was quite different than how we travel now. Although riding on donkeys might sound like fun, it would have taken a long time to get from one town to another. In the hot sun, with no windows to roll down or air conditioning to turn on, you can bet some of those dusty desert trips were pretty miserable.

How we get around now is nothing short of amazing. In four-and-a-half hours you can fly from the east coast to the west coast of the United States. Or you could drive. Or take a train or ride a bus. Because there are so many great ways to travel now, we have the opportunity to see more of God's great world and the people in it.

God, I am so grateful for the different ways of getting from here to there. Thank you for cars that have air conditioning and planes that cut down on travel time. When I start complaining about long trips, help me to remember how blessed I am to live in a world with great transportation.

Jump in the car and take the long road trip out of the maze.

End here

Act of Gratitude

I am thankful to God for transportation.

Here's what I am going to do this week
to show how grateful I am.

_____

_____

_____

_____

_____

_____

_____

_____

_____

TREEHOUSES

"Come to me, all you who are tired and are carrying heavy loads. I will give you rest."
MATTHEW 11:28 NIRV

Secured in the hefty branches of a tall oak tree is a wooden treehouse. Planks of wood nailed to the tree trunk create a ladder that leads to the door. Inside, pillows are scattered on the floor with books, games, and other toys. A Bible sits on a crate with a flashlight next to it: a telltale sign of what this private hut is typically used for.

Where do you go to get away with God? Do you know that spending quiet time with him is the perfect way to rest? He tells us that if we are tired and feel like we are carrying heavy loads, we should come to him. If you haven't already, find somewhere you can go to be alone with God. You won't regret it.

Thank you, God, for wanting to be with me. Thanks for giving me a place to go when I need to be alone with you. Help me to bring my cares and concerns to you when I need someone to talk to. I want to hear what you have to say.

DID YOU KNOW?

The world's largest treehouse is located in Crossville, Tennessee. It is also known as The Minister's Treehouse. It is 97 feet tall and is supported by a huge oak tree. It is made completely out of wood and has about 80 rooms, including a church and a bell tower.

Draw your own treehouse below!

Act of Gratitude

I am thankful to God for quiet places to meet with him.

Here's what I am going to do this week
to show how grateful I am.

_____

_____

_____

_____

_____

_____

_____

_____

_____

HOPES AND DREAMS

*"I say this because I know what I am planning
for you," says the LORD. "I have good plans for you,
not plans to hurt you. I will give you hope
and a good future."*

JEREMIAH 29:11 NCV

What excites you the most about growing up?
Do you know what you want to be, or what you'd
like to spend your life doing? God has put you on
this earth for a very special reason. He has things
planned for you. Good things! Great things!

It's okay if you aren't sure what you want to do with
your life yet. You can trust God to show you just
at the right moment. If you already have a plan,
hand it over to God and trust him to take care of
it. God knows you perfectly, and he is delighted to
work with you to accomplish more than you could
ever hope or dream.

Thank you, God, that you have a plan for my life.
You are good, and you have good things in store
for me. I hand my own plan over to you and ask
you to bless it or change it, whichever you know is
best for me. I trust your plans for me because
I trust you.

CHANGE ONE LETTER FROM THE PREVIOUS WORD AND WATCH AS PLAN TURNS INTO LIFE.

PLAN

_ _ _ _   what you do with friends or toys

_ _ _ _   how you communicate with God

_ _ _ _   something you use to carry food

_ _ _ _   a British streetcar

_ _ _ _   a group of people that makes up one side in a game

_ _ _ _   a line made by sewing two pieces of cloth together

_ _ _ _   something you can sit on

_ _ _ _   past tense of send

_ _ _ _   payment made to an owner for use

_ _ _ _   to talk excessively about something for a long time

_ _ _ _   to gasp for air

_ _ _ _   a plate of glass for a window

_ _ _ _   a marked path on a highway wide enough for one car

. _ _ _ _   a long straight mark made with a pen or pencil

LIFE

Act of Gratitude

I am thankful to God for hopes and dreams.

Here's what I am going to do this week
to show how grateful I am.

_____

_____

_____

_____

_____

_____

_____

_____

_____